TOP 10 TEAMS OF THE DECADE

SCHOLASTIC INC.

New York   Toronto   London   Auckland

Sydney   Mexico City   New Delhi   Hong Kong

Photos:

Front cover:

(Top left) © Christian Petersen/Getty Images; (top right) © Paul Bereswill/NBAE/Getty Images; (bottom left) © Nathaniel S. Butler/NBAE/Getty Images; (bottom middle) © ASSOCIATED PRESS; (bottom right) © Greg Nelson/ Sports Illustrated/Getty Images

Interior:

(Title page clockwise from top left) © Andrew D. Bernstein/ NBAE/Getty Images; © Jesse D. Garrabrant/NBAE/Getty Images; © Jim Rogash/Getty Images; © Andrew D. Bernstein/NBAE/Getty Images; (3 top; 5 upper right, bottom left; 6; 12 left; 14 bottom; 24 right) © Nathaniel S. Butler/NBAE/Getty Images; (3 bottom, 21 bottom right) © Victor Baldizon/NBAE/Getty Images; (4, 5 top left & background, 9 right, 10, 11 bottom left, 15 top & middle, 24 left) © Andrew D. Bernstein/NBAE/Getty Images; (5 bottom right, 18 left) © Manny Millan/Sports Illustrated/Getty Images; (7, 20 bottom) © Garrett Ellwood/NBAE/Getty Images; (8 left, 8-9 bottom) © Jeff Haynes/AFP/Getty Images; (9 left) © Noren Trotman/NBAE/Getty Images; (11 top, 23 top left, 29 bottom, 30) © Jesse D. Garrabrant/NBAE/Getty Images; (11 bottom right, 26 top) © Jed Jacobsohn/Getty Images; (12 bottom) © Ezra Shaw/Getty Images; (13, 26 bottom, 27 bottom) © Elsa/Getty Images; (14 top) © Joe Biever/Sports Illustrated/Getty Images; (15 bottom) © Noah Graham/NBAE/Getty Images; (16, 32 bottom left) © Getty Images; (17 top) © Stephen Dunn/Getty Images; (17 bottom left) © Terrence Vaccaro/Getty Images; (17 bottom right, 18 right) © Brian Bahr/Getty Images; (19) © Fernando Medina/NBAE/Getty Images; (20 top, 22) © Joe Murphy/NNBAE/Getty Images; (21 top) © Issac Baldizon/ Getty Images; (21 middle right) © Doug Benc/Getty Images; (21 bottom left) © Greg Nelson/Sports Illustrated/ Getty Images; (23 bottom, 29 top, 32 top right) © Ronald Martinez/Getty Images; (25, 27 top) © Jim Rogash/Getty Images; (PG 28) © John W McDonough/Sports Illustrated/Getty Images; (31; 32 middle left, middle right, bottom right) © Christian Petersen/Getty Images

ISBN 978-0-545-27943-7

© 2011 by NBA Properties, Inc.

12 11 10 9 8 7 6 5 4   11 12 13 14 15 16/0

Designed by Cheung Tai
Printed in the U.S.A.   40
First printing, January 2011

INTRODUCTION

The Lakers entered the 2010-11 season having won the previous two NBA titles. Their victory in the 2010 NBA Finals gave them five NBA championships in the previous 11 seasons. In 2011, they hope to win their 17th NBA crown, which would tie Los Angeles with Boston for the most league titles.

But they have some serious competition. The Heat's "Big Three" of Chris Bosh, LeBron James, and Dwyane Wade have teamed up in Miami to win NBA titles. Lots of them.

"Not two, not three, not four, not five, not six, not seven," James said in July 2010. "Hey, and when I say that, I really believe that. . . . We believe we can win multiple championships."

If James's prediction comes true, the Miami Heat will be one of the greatest teams in NBA history. But it is not easy to win one title, much less multiple championships. Miami's quest to become the team of *this* decade will begin by trying to overcome the Los Angeles Lakers, the team of the *last* decade.

"The Lakers are the champions and we know the Lakers are very good," said Wade. "That's the team that everyone's shooting for and they should be. Not the Miami Heat—the Los Angeles Lakers."

The Lakers weren't the only great team of the last decade. The San Antonio Spurs won three championships (2003, 2005, and 2007). The Celtics won the 2008 NBA title and nearly won another championship in 2010. Detroit won the 2004 NBA Finals and was a championship contender throughout the decade. As for the Heat, Wade led them to a championship in 2006.

As Bosh, James, and Wade try to build a dynasty in Miami, one thing is for sure: There will be 29 other NBA teams trying to stop them.

3

2000-01 LOS ANGELES LAKERS

After winning the 2000 NBA title, the Lakers took a well-deserved rest. Unfortunately for them, their rest extended into the next season.

Los Angeles stumbled out of the gate during the first half of the 2000-01 season. Eventually they regained their footing, and went on to win the Pacific Division title.

Los Angeles' hot streak continued in the 2001 NBA Playoffs. The Lakers swept Portland in three games and then won four straight against Sacramento to advance to the 2001 Western Conference Finals against San Antonio. The Spurs had swept the Lakers in the 1999 NBA Playoffs, and many picked San Antonio to win again.

But the Lakers, led by center Shaquille O'Neal and guard Kobe Bryant, avenged that 1999 defeat by sweeping the Spurs. They won Game 3 by 39 points, and closed the series with a 111-82 victory in Game 4. The sweep gave Los Angeles 19 straight victories, including 11 in a row in the playoffs.

4

2000-01 LOS ANGELES LAKERS

The Lakers' winning streak ended in Game 1 of the 2001 NBA Finals, when they lost in overtime to Philadelphia. But Los Angeles won the next four games to claim the NBA title. The Lakers finished the season having won 23 of their last 24 games, including a 15-1 mark in the postseason that set an NBA Playoff record.

"No team in Laker history has ever played at a higher level of perfection than this team," said Chick Hearn, the club's long-time broadcaster.

6

2001-02 LOS ANGELES LAKERS

The Lakers hoped to make history in 2002 by winning their third title in a row. Only three other teams in NBA history had done that. But it would not be easy.

Though Los Angeles (58-24) tied for the second-best record in the NBA, the club finished second in the Pacific Division to Sacramento (61-21). The Kings wanted revenge after losing to the Lakers in the 2000 and 2001 NBA Playoffs. They would get their chance in the 2002 Western Conference Finals, which turned out to be a classic seven-game series.

The Lakers won Game 1. Sacramento won the next two games, and in Game 4, the Kings built a 24-point lead in Los Angeles. The Lakers then put together one of the greatest comebacks in NBA Playoff history, capped by Robert Horry's three-pointer at the buzzer to win 100-99. Sacramento won Game 5, Los Angeles won Game 6, and the teams returned to Sacramento for Game 7, where the Lakers pulled out a 112-106 victory in overtime.

"This was the most highly contested series we've been in during this [three-year] run," said Lakers Coach Phil Jackson. "It's about

7

finishing games and doing whatever it takes. We were just not going to lose."

Los Angeles went on to sweep New Jersey in the 2002 NBA Finals. Jackson, who led the Bulls to six titles during the 1990s, had his third "three-peat" as a coach.

"It's my belief that the third [title] in three successive years is almost always the most unique and most difficult," said Jackson. "It certainly was this year."

2002-03 SAN ANTONIO SPURS

After winning their first NBA title in 1999, the Spurs expected more to follow. But injuries shortened their playoff run in 2000, and the Lakers ended their seasons in 2001 and 2002.

To overcome the Lakers, the Spurs added guards Tony Parker and Manu Ginobili. The two struggled at first, especially Parker, who was just 20 years old. But they improved later in the season, and the Spurs rolled to a 60-22 record, tied for the NBA's best in 2002-03.

After defeating Phoenix in six games, the Spurs faced the Lakers in the 2003 Western Conference Semifinals. This time, San Antonio got the better of Los Angeles, winning the series in six games.

"We had a tough couple of years with [the Lakers]," said Spurs Coach Gregg Popovich. "To finally play well enough is beyond comprehension."

The Spurs went on to defeat Dallas in the Western Conference Finals and then beat New Jersey in the 2003 NBA Finals. Forward Tim Duncan earned the NBA Finals MVP Award, and

center David Robinson concluded his brilliant 14-year career by winning his second NBA championship. He had 13 points and 17 rebounds in the final game.

"I'm just thrilled that David ended his career with a game like that," Popovich said. "His effort was really wonderful. He really dug down deep and showed how important it was to him to get help us get this victory."

2003-04 DETROIT PISTONS

Six new players. A new coach in Larry Brown. No superstars. The Pistons hardly had the look of a champion entering the 2003-04 season.

But champions they would become, thanks to a red-hot defense, a team-first attitude, and a midseason trade that brought in power forward Rasheed Wallace.

After posting a 54-28 record during the season, Detroit ousted Milwaukee in the First Round of the playoffs. The Pistons' championship run took them through New Jersey, which was seeking its third consecutive trip to the NBA Finals. Detroit bounced back from a heartbreaking triple-overtime loss in Game 5 to win Games 6 and 7, stunning the Nets.

The Pistons moved on to face Indiana in the Eastern Conference Finals. The Pacers had the NBA's best record in 2003-04, but they could not crack Detroit's defense. The Pistons limited Indiana to 72.7 points per game and won the series in six games.

In the 2004 NBA Finals, Detroit faced the Los Angeles Lakers. Again, nobody gave the Pistons a chance.

"We love it that nobody expects us to win, that us-against-the-world attitude. We've had it all year," said Detroit guard Richard Hamilton.

North Star Library
SLC School District

13

Again, the Pistons stunned everyone. The Pistons bottled up the Lakers' offense and won the series four games to one. Guard Chauncey Billups (21 points per game) won the NBA Finals MVP Award, but this was truly a team victory.

"We believed. We didn't worry about what people wrote [or] what was said on TV," said Hamilton. "We said to ourselves, 'Anything is possible if we play together as five on the offensive and defensive end.'"

14

2004-05 SAN ANTONIO SPURS

After losing to the Lakers in the 2004 NBA Playoffs, the Spurs entered the 2004-05 season determined to return to the NBA Finals. Though slowed by injuries after a hot start, San Antonio still finished 59-23, tied for the second-best mark in the league.

More important, the Spurs were healthy and ready to make another championship run. They defeated Denver (four games to one), Seattle (four games to two), and Phoenix (four games to one) to advance to the 2005 NBA Finals, where San Antonio faced Detroit.

Behind guard Manu Ginobili and forward Tim Duncan, the Spurs easily won the first two games. The Pistons, who were trying to win their second consecutive NBA title, dominated Games 3 and 4 in Detroit. In Game 5, Robert Horry's three-pointer in the final seconds of overtime gave San Antonio a 96-95 victory and a 3-2 series lead.

"He was so calm," Duncan said of Horry, who scored 21 points. "Put him in a big game in the fourth quarter, and he shows up. He's 'Big Shot Bob.'"

16

But the Pistons were not done. They won Game 6 at San Antonio to force a seventh and deciding game. In Game 7, the Spurs rallied from a nine-point deficit to defeat the Pistons 81-74. Duncan (25 points) and Ginobili (23 points) led the way as San Antonio won its third NBA title in seven seasons.

2005-06 MIAMI HEAT

The Heat nearly reached the 2005 NBA Finals, losing to the Detroit Pistons in the Eastern Conference Finals. So what did Miami President Pat Riley do? He remade the roster, surrounding center Shaquille O'Neal and guard Dwyane Wade with several new players.

"We were a minute and a half from the Finals. Big deal," Riley said in explaining his decision. "It's about winning a championship."

Riley's moves did not pay off at first, as Miami had an up-and-down season. Injuries, a coaching change (Riley returned as coach), and inconsistent play led to a 52-30 record.

But the Heat came together in the 2006 NBA Playoffs, defeating Chicago (four games to two), New Jersey (four games to one), and Detroit (four games to two). In the NBA Finals, however, the Heat stumbled badly, losing the first two games to the Dallas Mavericks and falling behind by 13 points with 6:34 to play in Game 3.

At that point, Wade took over the series and made history. He rallied Miami to a 98-96 victory, followed by an easy win in Game 4. In Game 5, Wade scored 43 points to propel Miami to a 101-100 victory in overtime and a 3-2 series lead. He continued his spectacular play in Dallas, scoring 36 points as Miami won 95-92

19

to complete the greatest comeback in NBA Finals history. Only the '69 Boston Celtics and the '77 Portland Trail Blazers overcame an 0-2 finals deficit to win the NBA title.

"That's what makes it so sweet, because not at one moment did one of us not believe," Wade said. "No matter what, in the locker room, it was 15 [players] strong."

2006-07 SAN ANTONIO SPURS

The Spurs won their fourth NBA title in nine seasons in 2007, and this may have been San Antonio's best team. Guards Manu Ginobili and Tony Parker gave the Spurs one of the NBA's top backcourts, while forward Tim Duncan continued to star as one of the league's best big men.

San Antonio had a 13-game winning streak during the regular season as the club finished with a 58-24 record, third best in the NBA. The Spurs won 25 of their last 31 regular-season games, and then posted a 16-4 record in the 2007 NBA Playoffs. San Antonio defeated Denver (four games to one), Phoenix (four games to two), and Utah (four games to one), finally going up against Cleveland (four games to none) to win the championship.

The Cavaliers, led by the seemingly unstoppable LeBron James, had reached the NBA Finals by upsetting the veteran Detroit Pistons. But the Spurs found a way to contain

James, capping their sweep with an 83-82 victory. Ginobili (27 points) and Parker (24 points) led the Spurs in Game 4. Parker, who averaged 24.5 points per game in the series, became the first European-born player to win the NBA Finals MVP Award.

"I put in a lot of work to get here," Parker said. "I'm speechless. When I look at the [MVP] trophy and wake up tomorrow, it's still going to be a dream."

2007-08 BOSTON CELTICS

Celtic Pride was officially back.

The Celtics put together their "Big Three" in the summer of 2007, when the team traded for guard Ray Allen and forward Kevin Garnett. Those two joined long-time Celtics star Paul Pierce to suddenly turn Boston into a title contender.

"A lot of people think you can just show up and get to the [NBA] Finals," Boston coach Doc Rivers said before the 2007-08 season. "That's not going to happen."

Boston's "Big Three" showed up ready to work. Allen, Garnett, and Pierce were hungry for a championship, and willing to make sacrifices to get their hands on the Larry O'Brien Trophy.

"Playing together is not going to be an issue. That's where basketball becomes fun," Allen said before the 2007-08 season. "Guys aren't fighting for anything but each other and for victories."

The Celtics, who had won just 24 games the season before, posted the NBA's best record (66-16) in 2007-08. Their 42-game improvement was the greatest one-season turnaround in NBA history.

25

2007-08
BOSTON CELTICS

Boston won with defense, allowing just 90.3 points per game during the regular season. In the 2008 NBA Playoffs, the Celtics' defense carried them through difficult series against Atlanta, Cleveland, and Detroit.

In the 2008 NBA Finals, Boston defeated the Los Angeles Lakers in six games, and hoisted its 17th championship banner, the most of any NBA team.

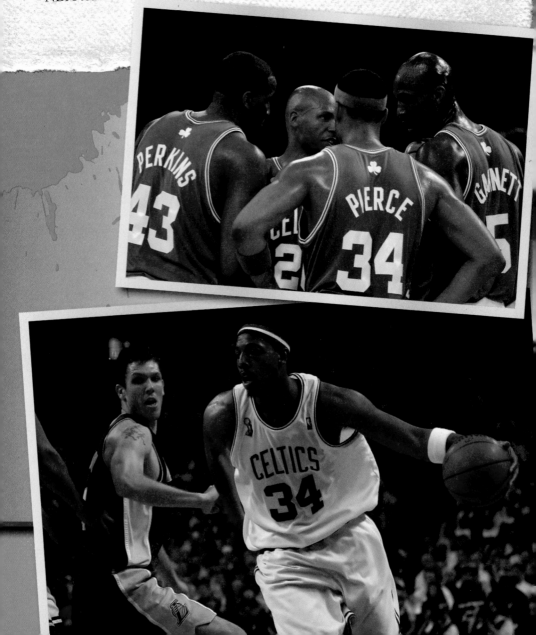

2008-09 LOS ANGELES LAKERS

It took seven years, but Kobe Bryant and the Lakers again stood atop the NBA.

Bryant and Shaquille O'Neal led Los Angeles to three consecutive NBA titles (2000-02), but after O'Neal was traded, the team struggled. The return of Phil Jackson as coach and a trade for center Pau Gasol helped the Lakers become title contenders. Their loss to Boston in the 2008 NBA Finals made it apparent they still needed to improve if they wanted to win a championship.

The Lakers did improve in 2008-09, posting the third-best

record (65-17) in franchise history. They had some surprising struggles against Houston and Denver in the 2009 NBA Playoffs, but they survived and advanced to play Orlando in the NBA Finals.

The Lakers won the first two games in Los Angeles, a blowout in Game 1 (100-75) and an overtime thriller (101-96) in Game 2. The Magic took Game 3 (108-104) in Orlando, but Derek Fisher's clutch shooting propelled Los Angeles to a 99-91 overtime victory in Game 4. The Lakers recorded an easy 99-86 victory in Game 5 to claim the 15th NBA title in franchise history.

The victory gave Jackson his 10th NBA championship, the most by any coach (he surpassed Red Auerbach, who had nine).

"He took his glasses off, threw his head back, and soaked it all in because this is a special time," Bryant said of Jackson. "For us to be the team that got him that historic 10th championship is special for us."

2009-10 LOS ANGELES LAKERS

Before the season, many predicted that the Boston Celtics and Los Angeles Lakers would meet in the 2010 NBA Finals. Nobody could have predicted the route each team would take.

Both teams struggled with injuries during the regular season. As the 2010 NBA Playoffs began, neither the Lakers nor the Celtics seemed headed for the Finals. But both made it. After defeating Miami, Boston went on to stun Cleveland and Orlando. Meanwhile, the Lakers survived a First Round test against Oklahoma City, swept Utah, and outlasted Phoenix to advance to their third straight NBA Finals.

Both teams had something to prove. Los Angeles wanted to show it could meet the challenge presented by the rugged Celtics, who had overpowered the Lakers in the 2008 NBA Finals. Boston wanted to win a second title in three years to establish itself as one of the decade's top teams.

The teams split the first two games in Los Angeles, but the Lakers reclaimed home-court advantage by winning Game 3 in Boston. After the Celtics won Games 4 and 5, the series returned to Los Angeles with Boston needing just one victory for the championship. The Lakers coasted to an easy victory in Game 6, forcing Game 7 to decide the championship.

31

2009-10
LOS ANGELES LAKERS

Boston led for most of Game 7, building a 13-point advantage in the third quarter. But the Lakers rallied, and several clutch plays in the final minutes propelled Los Angeles to an 83-79 victory. It was the first time the Lakers had defeated their arch-rivals in a Game 7.

"This one is by far the sweetest, because it's them," said Lakers guard Kobe Bryant. "[Beating the Celtics] meant the world to me, but I couldn't focus on that. I had to focus on playing."

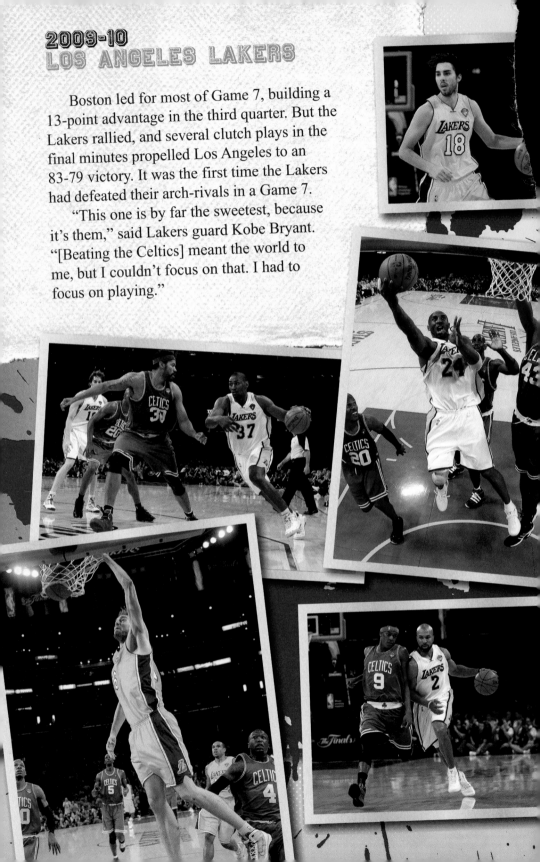